ISBN 978-0-265-01864-4
PIBN 11027633

1 MONTH OF
FREE
READING

at
www.ForgottenBooks.com

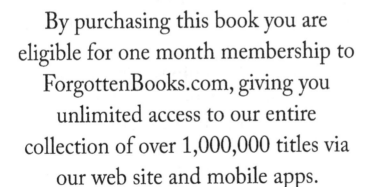

By purchasing this book you are eligible for one month membership to ForgottenBooks.com, giving you unlimited access to our entire collection of over 1,000,000 titles via our web site and mobile apps.

To claim your free month visit:
www.forgottenbooks.com/free1027633

Historic, Archive Document

Do not assume content reflect scientific knowledge, policies,

THE
WARREN
NURSERY

Plants, Seeds
Bulbs and Garden Supplies

69 WEST BROADWAY
NEW YORK, N. Y.
Phone Walker 9779

To Our Friends and Customers

WE present our Catalog for 1926. You will find herein only first quality goods of every description sold with the guarantee that they grow or we will gladly make good our promise. It has been our aim for many years to please our customers at all times, giving them only the healthiest and the best of growing plants, Fruit Trees, Berry Plants, Shrubs, Trees, Evergreens, Bulbs, Seeds and all garden supplies at the most reasonable prices.

We are deeply grateful to those who have helped us grow, and for their confidence in our sincerity of purpose and their faith in our ability to serve them. Thanking you for the opportunity of serving you in 1926,

Yours very truly,

THE WARREN NURSERY.

FRUIT TREES

APPLE.—Extra fine stock of the best quality, vigorous, full of vitality.

Prices 85c to $1.50, according to age and size.

Dwarf trees bear sooner and are excellent for small gardens as they do not grow large. Price $1.25 each.

Baldwin	R. I. Greening
Delicious	Spitzenberg
Grimes' Golden	Winesap
Jonathan	Wealthy
Northern Spy	Yellow Transparent

PEAR.—These are fine healthy trees.

Price $1.10 to $1.75, according to age, size and variety.

Dwarf trees $1.40 each.

Bartlett	Kieffer
Clapp's Favorite	Seckel

CHERRY.—Big robust trees will bear fruit in a short time.

Price, Sweet Cherry, $1.25 to $2.00. Sour(s) Cherry, $1.10 to $1.75.

Black Tartarian	Windsor
Gov. Wood	Yellow Spanish
Napoleon's Biggareau	Early Richmond(s)
Schmidt's Biggareau	May Duke(s)
Montmorency(s)	

PLUM.—Extra fine trees ready to grow. Price $1.25 to $2.00, according to size.

Abundance	Lombard
German Prune	Reine Claude
Shippers' Pride	

APRICOT.—One of the finest fruit trees to grow.

Price $1.50 each.

Alexander

QUINCE.—Every garden should have at least one.

Price $1.50 and $1.75.

Champion   Orange

PEACH.—These trees are the best grown.
Price 60c to $1.25.

Champion	Elberta
Crawford Early	Iron Mountain
Crawford Late	J. H. Hale

FIG.—Price $1.00 each.

Celestiale

GRAPE.—Price 25c to 50c.

Concord	Niagara
Champagne (75c)	Catawba

SMALL FRUITS

BLACKBERRY—Price $1.50 per doz.

Eldorado   Blower   Bushel

CURRANT.—Price 25c and 35c.

Cherry Red   Fay's Prolific   White Grape

GOOSEBERRY.—Price 25c and 35c.

Houghton   Downing

RASPBERRY—Price 75c., $1.00 and $1.50 a dozen.

Cuthbert   Cumberland (Bl^a_{ck} Cap)
St. Regis

ORNAMENTAL SHRUBS
Price 50c to $1.50, according to size and age.

FLOWERING SHRUBS
Althea (Rose of Sharon)—all colors.
Amygdalus (Flowering Almond)—White and Pink.
Buddleia (Butterfly Bush)—Lavender.
Calycanthus (Sweet Scented Shrub).
Deutzia Crenata Rosea—Pink.
Deutzia Pride of Rochester—White.
Forsythia Golden Bells.
Hydrangea Aborescens (Hills of Snow).
Hydrangea Paniculata Grandiflora.
Lilac—White and Purple.
Lilac (French)—Charles X—Purple. Louis Spath—Lavender. Madame Lemoine—Double White. Marie Legray—White.
Lonicera (Honeysuckle Upright)—Pink, Red, White.
Philadelphus (Mock Orange).
Spirea Anthony Waterer.
Spirea Froebelli.
Spirea Obulifolia Aurea.
Spirea Von Houtteii.
Symphoricarpus Racemosus (White Snowberry).
Viburnum (Snowball).
Viburnum Opulus (Common Snowball).
Viburnum Dentatum (Arrowwood).
Viburnum Plicatum (Japan Snowball).
Weigelia Eva Rathke—Red.
Weigelia Rosea—Pink.
Weigelia Variegated—Green and Gold leaf.

TREE FORM
Betchel's Flowering Crab.
Double Flowering Peach—Red and White.

Flowering Plum.

Hydrangea.

Rose Trees.

We have an exceptional fine lot of this stock in several sizes and ages and feel sure we can satisfy your wants.

VINES

Prices, 35c to 75c.

Ampelopsis—Boston Ivy.

Clematis—Paniculata (small white flower).

Clematis—Jackmannii (purple large flower).

Clematis—Hewryii (white large flower).

Clematis—Mme. Edward Andre (red large flower).

Honeysuckle—Japanese.

Dutchman's Pipe.

EVERGREENS

These are all nursery-grown plants cut back to insure good bushy, healthy trees and for vigor and vitality cannot be duplicated anywhere at our low prices. Prices are from 90 cents up, according to size, age, variety and species.

Arborvitæ—Pyramid.

Arborvitæ—Globe Shape.

Arborvitæ—Tom Thumb.

Biota Aurea Nana.

Black Hill Spruce.

Douglas Fir.

Canada Hemlock.

Juniper Argentia.

Norway Spruce.

Retinospora Plumosa.

Retinospora Plumosa Aurea.

Retinospora Pisifera Aurea.

BROAD-LEAVED EVERGREENS

Rhododendrons   Laurels

Azaleas

TREES

Umbrella Trees.................$1.50 to $2.50
Weeping Mulberry.............. 2.75 to 3.50
Magnolia Trees................. 1.00 to 1.50

ROSES

We have over fifty varieties of everblooming and perpetual hardy roses in an assortment of grades and ages and feel sure we can supply every rose lover's wants. Prices from 25 cents.

CLIMBING ROSES

American Beauty   Flowers of Fairfield
American Pillar   Gardenia
Blue Rambler   Orleans
Christine Wright   Paul's Scarlet Climber
Doctor Van Fleet   Showers of Gold
Dorothy Perkins   Silver Moon
Excelsa   Tausendschon

Yellow Rambler

HEDGE PLANTS

CALIFORNIA PRIVET.—Nice healthy plants, full of branches and lots of roots. All 2 years old and over.

Prices $2.50 per 100 to $7.00 per 100.

BARBERRY—Stocky, bushy plants with good root systems, 3 and 4 years old.

Price $7.00 per 100 and up.

Many of the flowering shrubs make excellent hedge, such as the Spireas, Mock Orange and Rose of Sharon. Come in and consult us about it.

PERENNIALS

These are nice large plants. Some are 3 year clumps, all of which will flower the same year as planted.

Prices 15c to 35c each.

Aquilegia or Columbine   Lily of the Valley
Coreopsis   Phlox—all colors
Chrysanthemum   Peonies
Delphinium   Physostegia
Hardy Lilies   Shasta Daisy
Gallardia   Tritoma
Iris—German   Uka
Iris—Japanese   Hollyhocks

BULBS—TUBERS—ROOTS

GLADIOLUS.—All first grade, large bulbs, sure to flower.

	Doz.
America, Pink	$0.40
Chicago White—White	.50
Halley, Salmon	.50
Mrs. Francis King, Flame	.50
Mrs. Frank Pendelton, Pink and Red	.50
Mrs. Watt, Wine Red	.75
Nora, Blue	.90
Peace, White and Lavender	.60
Prince of Wales, Salmon	.75
Schwaben, Canary Yellow	.65
Willie Wigman, Blush Pink and Red	.75
Mixed, All Fine Colors	.30

DAHLIAS.—We have a good selection of colors to choose from at from 25c. to 50c. a large field clump.

We can also furnish you the finest named varieties 10 to 25 per cent. lower than the average low price. Let us have your order.

and 50c.

Lilium Magnificum, Red Lily.

Lilium Rubrum, Crimson Lily.

Lilium Aratum, Gold-banded Lily of Japan.

These are perfectly hardy, coming up year after year and multiplying.

CANNAS.—

	Doz.
City of Portland, Finest Pink	$1.00
Florence Vaughn, Yellow	.60
Louisiana, Red	.60
Pennsylvania, Red	.60
Red King Humbert, Red Leaf, Red Flower	1.00
The President, Finest Red	1.00
Venus, Yellow and Pink Spots	.60
Wyoming, Bronze Leaf, Orange Flower	.60
Yellow King Humbert, Yellow	1.00

PEONIES.—35c. to $1.00, according to size. Red, Pink and White.

We can also supply named varieties at the lowest prices.

TUBEROSES.—Double Pearl. 60c. a dozen to $1.00 a dozen, according to size.

LILY OF THE VALLEY or May Bells.
Pips or individual Plants..........25 for 50c.
Field Clumps ....25c. each

OXALIS.—Mixed, 20c. a dozen, 3 dozen for 50c.

ASPARAGUS ROOTS.—$2.50 and $3.00 per 100, 3-year-old.

RHUBARB.—10c. to 50c. a root, according to size.

HORSERADISH ROOTS.—50c. a dozen.

SEEDS.—We carry a full line of well-known flower and vegetable seed.

GRASS SEED.—Our own Warren Brand Lawn Seed has proven wonderfully satisfactory to all who have used it.

Quart	$0.25
2 lb. Bag	.60
5 lb. Bag	1.50
10 lb. Bag	3.00
100 lb. Bag	27.00

All kinds of bedding and vegetable plants in season.

FERTILIZER

POTASH MARL.—20c. a quart; $2.50-100 lbs.

SHEEP MANURE.—

5 lbs.	$0.40
10 lbs.	.80
25 lbs.	1.50
100 lbs.	3.50

BONE MEAL.—

5 lbs.	$0.45
10 lbs.	.85
100 lbs.	4.00

SPRAY MATERIALS to kill insects and disease.

Hammond's Slugshot   Bordeaux Lead
Bordeaux Mixture   Arsenate of Lead
 (Paste and Powder)   Kerosene Emulsion
Black Leaf "40"   Tobacco Dust
Preventol for Flys and Mosquitoes
Tanglefoot Roach and Ant Powder, Etc.

MISCELLANEOUS GOODS

Bamboo Stakes   Plant Stakes
For Dahlias, Tomatoes, Etc.
Bamboo Rakes for raking old grass, leaves, etc., off lawns.
Plant labels for marking varieties, etc.

SPECIALS

One Dozen Flowering Shrubs, 2 to 3 feet high.

$5.00

3 Clumps of Dahlias and 25 Choice Mixed Gladiolus.

$1.00

5 Hardy Everblooming Roses
Five Varieties

$1.25

2 Clumps of Dahlias   12 Gladiolus
12 Cannas

$1.00

2 Aquilegia   2 Coreopsis
2 Shasta Daisy   2 Phlox

$1.00

12 Gladiolus   2 Perennials
6 Cannas   6 Tuberoses

$1.00

1 Pyramid Arborvitæ, 15 inches high
1 Norway Spruce, 15 inches high
1 Globe Arborvitæ, 15 inches high

Package of Sheep Manure to Fer-
tilize above trees

$5.00

1 Apple Tree	2 Currant Bushes or
1 Pear Tree	Gooseberry Bushes
2 Grape Vines	2 Raspberry Plants

$3.00

2 Hardy Lilies	2 Peonies

$1.00

5 Choice Peach Trees

$2.50

CPSIA information can be obtained
at www.ICGtesting.com
Printed in the USA
BVHW04s1224011018
528938BV00023B/1222/P